MIKE YOUNG

AND TEX'S MAGIC SPELL

Illustrations by
Tom Bailey and David Blake

Muller, Blond & White

Everybody loves teddy bears. We hug them and talk to them and sometimes it almost seems as if they can talk back. SuperTed felt like this about his own teddy bear and took it with him wherever he went.

Sometimes this annoyed his friend, Spottyman. When they were on holiday in the West Indies, Spotty complained when SuperTed kept moving his teddy bear around on the beach.

"I'm just moving this deckchair out of the sun, Spotty." explained SuperTed. "It's my teddy. I think he's a bit hot."

"Don't be silly," his spotty friend replied. "Teddy bears don't feel the heat."

"*I* feel the heat," said SuperTed. "Why shouldn't he?"

Neither of them knew that, in a shack not far from the beach, Bulk and Skeleton were trying to cast a wicked spell on SuperTed. They were clipping clothes-pegs on to a tattered old teddy bear.

"Hocus pocus, locusts on a crocus," they whispered.

While they were doing this, the door crashed open and Texas Pete strode into the room. "Hey, dummies!" he yelled. "What are you doing?"

"It's magic," said Skeleton, jumping up and down.

"When we stick a clothes-peg on this teddy bear's arm . . .," added Bulk.

". . . SuperTed feels a pain in *his* arm." Skeleton completed the sentence gleefully.

Texas Pete was not impressed. "If you really want to cast an evil spell on SuperTed, you'll have to get hold of SuperTed's own personal teddy bear!" he cackled.

SuperTed and Spotty knew nothing of Texas Pete's wicked plans, of course. They were snuggling into their sleeping bags on the beach, watching the last embers of their campfire die down.

SuperTed smiled and gazed up at the stars. "This island is so peaceful, Spotty," he sighed. "You wouldn't think that the people who live here believe in evil spells and demons."

Spotty was startled. "Demons! You never told me there were demons!"

"There aren't any, really," said SuperTed, reassuringly. "Demons don't exist, and even if they do, I feel quite safe here, snuggling up to my teddy bear . . ." With that, he fell fast asleep.

SuperTed and Spotty slept so soundly that they did not notice two figures creep out from the trees that lined the beach.

Bulk and Skeleton had dressed in grass skirts and big, ugly masks. They had decided they would pretend to be demons and scare SuperTed and Spotty away. They tiptoed carefully towards the sleeping friends.

"Tippy toe," whispered Skeleton.

"Tippety tippety toe," whispered Bulk.

Then they jumped up and down in front of the two sleeping friends and made frightening noises. "Abadababadaba!"

Spotty and SuperTed woke up with a start. "By the Craters of Capricorn!" yelled Spotty in panic. "Demons!"

SuperTed was not so easily taken in. He chased the two figures across the beach and watched them disappear into the trees.

But when he got back to his sleeping bag, he had a nasty surprise. His spotty teddy bear was missing.

While SuperTed and Spotty were busy chasing Bulk and Skeleton, Texas Pete had crept out of the shadows and taken the teddy bear.

As he made his way back to the wooden shack, he was joined by Bulk and Skeleton, out of breath, and covered in mud and leaves. They had lost their masks.

Meanwhile, SuperTed was terribly upset. He was very fond of his teddy bear and could not understand what had happened to it. Spotty promised to help him find it so they both walked along the beach, peering carefully at every patch of sand.

Suddenly, Spotty threw up his arms in surprise. "By the Bald Birds of Spot! What's this?" he cried as he picked up the masks that Bulk and Skeleton had dropped.

SuperTed shook his head knowingly. "They're masks, Spotty. I think someone is doing some very bad magic."

In his shack, Tex was calling out all the nasty things he wanted to happen to SuperTed.

"Sting him with rattlers!" he shouted.

"Oh, yeah!" cried Bulk and Skeleton.

"Pester him with pins and needles!" screamed Texas Pete.

"Oh yeah, yeah, yeah!" moaned Bulk and Skeleton.

"Pain him with thunder and lightning!" blabbered Tex.

"Oh yeah, yeah, yeah, yeah!" wailed Bulk and Skeleton as they started to beat on two huge drums.

As soon as the sound of the drums drifted to the beach, SuperTed began to feel ill. He clutched his stomach and sat down with a bump.

"Oh, Spotty," he said, in a very slow, drowsy voice, "something very strange is happening to me . . ." Then he stretched himself out stiffly on the sand. "I think it's got something to do with the drumming . . .oh . . ."

Spotty quickly put on his rocket pack. "Don't worry, SuperTed, I'll put a stop to that horrible noise," he said, and he flew into the air and over the palm trees. Soon he saw Tex's shack, half-hidden in the trees beneath him.

With a burst from his rocket pack, he flew down and landed gently on the roof.

Inside, Texas Pete was laying out SuperTed's spotty teddy on a large wooden table. Bulk and Skeleton beat on the drums and moaned in a strange, tuneless way.

"Ooh! That sounds horrible," said Spotty, as he peered through a flap in the roof. "Anyone who heard that noise *would* feel ill!"

Texas Pete leaned menacingly over the teddy bear. He licked his lips and rolled his eyes. He was planning something really nasty.

At that moment, a plank in the roof came loose, and Spotty fell through the ceiling with a clatter. He fell right over Tex's shoulders. As Tex whirled around in panic, Spotty snatched the teddy bear from the table.

At that very moment SuperTed began to feel better.

"Oh! Thank goodness!" said SuperTed, gasping with relief. "Where's Spotty? I must find him. I'd better say my secret magic word."

A few seconds later, his cape flapping in the wind, the magic teddy bear flew over the palm trees and down towards Tex's shack.

Meanwhile, Bulk and Skeleton were tying up Spotty. Tex had picked up the spotty teddy bear and was making it fly through the air. Then he decided to make it crash.

At the same time that the spotty teddy hit Tex's table, SuperTed came crashing through the roof of the shack. Then the fur really began to fly, as the brave bear struggled with each of the villains in turn. He hurled Tex against the wall with so much force that the whole shack shuddered, but as he turned to pick up his teddy bear, the wicked cowboy slipped out into the night.

SuperTed dashed after him. They raced through the tropical ferns and palms of the island. For a moment, SuperTed thought he saw Tex hiding in the lush undergrowth, but when he pushed back the leaves, he saw a hideous mask.

"Blistering Bananas!" he gasped, and his heart beat with fear. He soon recovered and ran towards the beach. He could see Tex running across the sand in the moonlight, so he raced after him in a flash.

Tex did not stand a chance. A few moments later he was half-buried in the sand, with seaweed piled high over his head and shoulders.

SuperTed left him there and went back to set Spotty free. Spotty was very relieved to see him.

"I don't know what came over me on the beach," said SuperTed. "I think it must have been a bad attack of cramp."

The next day, SuperTed relaxed on the beach with his teddy bear safe beside him again. Spotty came towards him with three ice-creams.

"Thanks, Spotty," said SuperTed. "But why have you brought three?"

"One for you, one for me, and one for him," said Spotty, pointing to the spotty teddy bear.

"Don't be silly, Spotty," said SuperTed with a grin. "He can't eat an ice-cream, he's only a teddy bear." With that, he took two of the ice-creams out of Spotty's hands and started to lick them both.

Books in the SuperTed series

SuperTed and the Pothole Rescue
SuperTed and the Blue Whales
SuperTed Kicks up the Dust
SuperTed and Tex's Magic Spell
SuperTed and Bulk's Story
SuperTed in SuperTed's Dream
SuperTed and the Lumberjacks
SuperTed and Mother Nature
SuperTed Meets Zappy and Zoppy
SuperTed and the Green Planet
SuperTed at the Bottom of the Sea
SuperTed and the Hungry Monkeys
SuperTed and the Crystal Ball
SuperTed and the Gun Smugglers
SuperTed in the Arctic